Cambridge English Readers
....
Level 1

Series editor: Philip Prowse

Just Like a Movie

Sue Leather

CAMBRIDGE UNIVERSITY PRESS

Cambridge, New York, Melbourne, Madrid, Cape Town, Singapore, São Paulo

Cambridge University Press
The Edinburgh Building, Cambridge CB2 2RU, UK

www.cambridge.org
Information on this title: www.cambridge.org/9780521788137

First published 2000
7th printing 2006

Illustrations by Debbie Hinks

Printed in the United Kingdom at the University Press, Cambridge

A catalogue record for this publication is available from the British Library

ISBN-13 978-0-521-78813-7 paperback
ISBN-10 0-521-78813-7 paperback

ISBN-13 978-0-521-68630-3 paperback plus audio CD pack
ISBN-10 0-521-68630-X paperback plus audio CD pack

For Jan, who loves the movies

Contents

Chapter 1   Gina   5

Chapter 2   Carrie   10

Chapter 3   Two lives   16

Chapter 4   Lake Ontario   21

Chapter 5   Just like a movie   24

People in the story

Brad Black: a handyman. He loves the movies.
Gina: Brad's girlfriend. A school teacher.
Carrie: a rich girl.
Joe Rufino: a man in prison.

Places in the story

Chapter 1 *Gina*

I love the movies. New movies, old movies. I went to the movies a lot in Toronto. And it all started when I met Gina at the movies.

Gina! We met in October. Four years ago. We met outside a cinema. There was no snow but it was cold. It's cold in Toronto in fall. I was there to buy a ticket for a movie. It was *Forrest Gump*. She was there too, and we started to talk. Just like that.

'Hi,' I said, 'do you live around here?'

'Yes, I do. I live very near here,' she said.

'Do you? Me too,' I said.

She was nice. Really nice. I liked her smile. She gave me her telephone number. Before she went, she said, 'Oh, you didn't tell me your name.' I laughed.

'My name's Brad, Brad Black.'

I phoned her the next day. 'Why don't you come out with me?' I asked. 'To Salvo's Italian restaurant. It's cheap but nice. The spaghetti's very good.'

'Mmm, I love Italian food. My mum's Italian, you know. I love spaghetti,' she said. I was surprised. Really surprised. She was beautiful.

I went to her house at 7.30, to the address she gave me. We lived in the same area of the city. The poor area. She lived with her mother, who was old and sometimes sick. I went in the house to wait for Gina.

'Look after my daughter,' her mother said to me.

'Sure,' I said. I smiled my best smile. My good boy smile. Her mother looked at me. Was I good for her daughter? I was wearing my new shirt and pants. I looked good. Handsome. Black hair and blue eyes. She smiled at me.

Gina and I went to Salvo's. From that night it was our restaurant, our place. I started seeing her a lot. We fell in love. We were happy. I mean, really happy. Like in a movie. Like in *Love Story*. I loved that movie. I saw it five times.

Three months later we went to Salvo's restaurant again. I said, 'Gina, I love you. I want to marry you . . . but we need more money.' We were so happy, but we had no money. I was a handyman and I didn't make much money. And Gina was a teacher of small children. She was poor too.

Gina wanted to marry me. 'Brad,' said Gina, 'money's not important. We're poor, but we're happy.'

'But, Gina,' I said, 'if we want to get married and have children, we need money. We need a car, clothes, a beautiful house in Paris.'

I saw Paris in the movies and I wanted to live there. Gina smiled.

Gina and I talked a lot about money. Gina always smiled

at me. She was happy, but I wanted everything. Just like in the movies.

'I'm a handyman,' I said. 'I'm not a rich man! How can I make a lot of money?'

Like I told you, I like old movies. Gina and I went to the cinema every week. Every Saturday night. One Saturday we went to see a movie called *Dead Money*. It was about a man and a woman. Poor, just like us.

This man and woman, they had an idea, a very good idea. Well . . . she had the idea. She knew a man, another man. He was really rich but very old and sick. This man liked her. He was lonely. She married him. Then, about six months later, he died suddenly. She got all his money. It was millions of dollars. She got the money and married her young boyfriend. Happy ever after!

After the movie, we went for a drink.

'That's it!' I said to Gina. 'That's it, Gina! We can get money like that.'

Gina looked at me and smiled. 'Please, Brad,' she said, 'don't say those things. Money isn't everything!'

'But, Gina,' I said, 'how can you say that? We must have money!'

Gina looked at me again. She didn't smile. 'Listen to me, Brad,' she said. 'It's just a movie. It's just a stupid movie.'

Stupid eh? Well, maybe it wasn't so stupid. I thought about it a lot.

Then one day I met Carrie.

Chapter 2 *Carrie*

I'm a handyman, like I told you. I mean, I *was* a handyman. I worked on houses and office buildings in Toronto. Hard work and not a lot of money. Well, one day I did some work in Rosedale, the rich area of Toronto. Really rich. I was at a house. Carrie's house. I met her there. It was a big house, very big and very beautiful. She was very rich. She had millions.

'Hello,' I said to her. I smiled my best smile. My nice smile. I'm handsome, you know. Black, black hair. 'Black like your name,' Gina always said. Yeah, black hair, blue eyes and white teeth. Yeah, handsome.

'Hi,' the girl said and smiled. She was pretty and blonde. I like girls with black hair like Gina. But she was rich, this girl.

'I'm the handyman,' I said. 'I'm here to fix your roof.'

'Oh, yes,' she said. 'Come in.' She smiled at me. A pretty smile. Well, I knew she liked me. It was easy really. She was rich but she was lonely. I knew she was lonely.

After I finished my work, she said, 'Would you like some coffee?'

'Sure,' I said. We sat and talked in her kitchen. We talked for an hour. We drank coffee. I knew she liked me. She smiled a lot. I smiled too.

'You have a lovely house,' I said.

She looked happy and said, 'Thanks.'

'Really beautiful,' I said, 'like you.' Her face went red. I knew she liked it. All women like that.

'Do you have any family?' I asked Carrie.

'No,' she said. 'My parents died in a car accident ten years ago. I had an aunt, but she died last year. No sisters or brothers. I don't have any family.' Her face was sad.

It was good. Real good. I almost smiled, but I made a sad face too. Before I left her house, I said, 'Would you like to go out to dinner with me?'

I looked at her with my big blue eyes. She said, 'Yes.'

I didn't tell Gina about Carrie. I loved Gina, but we needed Carrie's money.

Two days later, Carrie and I went to a restaurant. Oh, not our restaurant, not the Italian one that Gina and I go to. Just a little Greek restaurant near Carrie's house.

'Where do you work?' I asked her.

'Oh, I don't really need to work,' she said. 'My parents died and they left me a lot of money.' I looked at her like I didn't know. 'Oh, you know, sometimes I help in the school. With the children. But only because I like it.' She smiled at me.

The waiter came with the bill. I looked at it. It was expensive. Eighty dollars.

'I want to pay,' said Carrie.

'No,' I said, 'I asked you to come . . .'

'Listen,' said Carrie, 'I know you're poor. It's OK. I like you. I want to pay.'

'Well . . . OK.' I smiled.

At the end of the evening I said, 'Come out with me again, Carrie. I really like you.'

'Sure,' she said, and smiled.

Carrie and I went out together for three months. It was difficult, because of Gina. I loved Gina. Everything was for Gina, but I knew I couldn't tell her about Carrie. About the money. One night I went out with Carrie, the next night I went out with Gina.

I only loved Gina, but I was nice to Carrie. Kind, you know. I sent her flowers. I gave her chocolates. After three months I gave her a ring. It was cheap, but she liked it.

'Oh, it's so beautiful!' she said. 'You're so good to me!'

'Carrie,' I said, 'I want to marry you.' She was so happy.

'Oh, yes . . . yes!!!' she said.

She didn't want expensive things or money. She was very rich. She had too much money. She only wanted love.

I didn't want to marry Carrie, but I wanted her money. I couldn't tell Gina about Carrie.

'Where are you going?' Gina asked one day.

'Oh, to see my friend Todd,' I said. Gina often stayed at home with her sick mother. She couldn't come with me. I knew I had to marry Carrie. Then kill her. For the money, you know. Just like in the movie. Like *Dead Money*. But I needed time. I needed three months . . .

'Gina,' I said, 'I've got to go to Vancouver for three months. I've got a job there.' Vancouver was far away from Toronto.

'Oh, Brad,' said Gina, 'I want to come with you.'

'No, Gina,' I said quickly. 'You've got to stay here. You've got to look after your mother. It's not a long time. I'll telephone you every day.' I kissed her. 'I can make some money in Vancouver. Then we can get married.'

Gina smiled. 'I want to marry you, Brad,' she said, 'but we don't need money.' I didn't listen and Gina and I said goodbye.

Then Carrie and I got married.

Chapter 3   *Two lives*

How could I kill Carrie? In the movie, it was easy. In *Dead Money* the husband was old and sick. But Carrie wasn't old and she wasn't sick. She was young. It was difficult. 'Wait and see,' I said to myself. 'Wait for an answer.' My life became more and more difficult.

Two lives. Like an actor. I stayed in Rosedale, in Toronto. I didn't go out much. I read a book about Vancouver. I phoned Gina every day from a phone box in Toronto.

'How's Vancouver?' she asked me.

'Oh, fine. Nice mountains. But I want to see you again,' I said. I was worried.

'How can I kill Carrie?' I asked myself. A month passed.

Two months. My life was very difficult. I didn't love Carrie; I loved Gina. Then one day I had a good idea. A really good idea. The weather was really bad. It was very windy and I needed to fix the roof of the house again.

'Please come and help me on the roof, Carrie,' I said.

'No, Brad,' she said. 'I can't. I'm afraid.'

'Oh please, Carrie. It's easy. I'll help you,' I said.

She smiled and said, 'OK.'

I saw this in a movie too. In *High Drama*. A man wants to kill his girlfriend, to get her money. The guy takes the girl on the roof and then kills her. The police think she falls, but he kills her.

'Come with me, Carrie,' I said. I took the ladder and we climbed up on the roof. Carrie was behind me. She gave me the tools. Then suddenly I fell back a little so that my hand touched the ladder.

'Oh, it's very windy here,' I said to Carrie. I pushed the ladder again.

'Brad,' she shouted, 'stop pushing the ladder. I'll fall!' But I pushed down more.

'I'm sorry, Carrie. It's so windy!' But then she moved a little and I fell back. I almost fell off the roof, but I didn't. Then we climbed down the ladder.

'I'm sorry,' I said to Carrie when we were in the house. 'It's just so windy.'

It worked in the movie, but it didn't work for me! I didn't know what to do. I had to kill Carrie. And quickly!

Then, two days later, Carrie went. I didn't do anything. I came home and she wasn't there. I looked everywhere. 'Carrie!' I shouted. I ran all over the house. I looked in the garden. I looked upstairs.

'Carrie, where are you?'

Maybe she was in the city, shopping. She often went shopping. I waited. She didn't come back.

That night I phoned the police. They came to the house and asked me a lot of questions.

'When did you last see your wife?'

'Where does she usually go?'

'Does she have friends?'

'Does she have family?'

'Did you have a fight with her yesterday?'

'Were you and your wife happy?'

So many questions! Just like in the movies. I didn't know where Carrie was. I just answered their questions. I told them we were happy.

When they left I didn't phone Gina. The police were watching me. I knew that, from the movies. Lucky I watch a lot of movies. It was better to wait. I waited and waited.

A week later the police came back to the house. 'There's a killer in Rosedale, Mr Black,' they said. 'There are three women dead.' They thought that he was Carrie's killer too. My face was sad.

'But where is she? Her body . . .' I said. 'What about her body?'

'We don't know, Mr Black,' said the police officer. 'We just don't know . . . but maybe the lake . . . maybe we'll never find your wife's body.'

I cried like they do in the movies. Like an actor. It was easy. I put my head in my hands and cried.

I knew I just had to wait. Wait for the money. But I didn't want to wait! There was a lot of money in the bank. Carrie didn't have any family, only me. The money was mine, but I couldn't wait. I wanted to marry Gina.

That night I went to bed and thought about the money. How could I get Carrie's money? Then, before I went to sleep, I saw the answer. On the little table next to the bed I saw her pen. Carrie's beautiful silver pen. And on the pen was her name: Carrie Black.

Chapter 4 *Lake Ontario*

The next day I put Carrie's pen in my pocket and I went to the lake. The weather was good and there were a lot of people near the lake. I sat down and looked at the water. Then I put the pen near the water, but not too near. Nobody saw me. I went home. Now I could only wait.

I didn't wait a long time. The next day at five o'clock in the afternoon, I had a telephone call. It was the police.

'Mr Black, I'm afraid we have some bad news,' said the policeman. 'Someone found your wife's pen near the lake. They saw her name in the newspaper, so they knew it was hers.'

'Oh,' I said. 'So . . . she's dead?'

'Well, Mr Black,' said the policeman, 'it looks really bad.'

I put the phone down and smiled. The police thought Carrie was dead!

The money was mine! But I had a problem, a big problem. The money. How could I tell Gina that I had so much money now?

I saw a movie about a poor American guy. It was called *Fat Cats*. This guy didn't know that he had an aunt who lived in England. She was very rich. She died and all her money was his. Millions. She didn't have any children, only cats. She left all her money to her poor American nephew, and the cats.

I telephoned Gina. 'Gina!' I said. 'We're rich! We don't have to worry about money now. I'm coming back from Vancouver. My rich aunt has died and I have millions of dollars!'

Gina laughed. 'That's wonderful, Brad! We can get married.'

'Yes,' I said, 'we can. I'll get the money and we'll buy a beautiful house in Paris. We're rich, Gina!'

I went to the bank in the city and sent the money to a bank in Paris. I bought two plane tickets, Toronto to Paris. I was so happy! So much money!!

A few days later I met Gina and we took a taxi to the airport. The sun was shining. We were rich! We were going to Paris! Happy ever after!

Chapter 5 *Just like a movie*

'It's good. Really good!' said Joe Rufino. Rufino was my friend in prison. My only friend.

'It's a great love story, Brad. I really like it . . . but . . . why are you here?' he asked. 'Why are you in prison? What happened to the happy ending?'

I smiled sadly at Rufino. Happy endings were nice in the movies. But the ending wasn't so nice for me. I was in prison. For five years. I started to tell him the story. All the story.

'Well, everything was like I told you. In the story, I mean. But there's more. Gina and I arrived at the airport, at departures. We checked in. Then we waited for the plane. Then two policemen walked towards us.'

'Are you Brad Black?' asked one of them.

'Yes,' I said.

'We want to talk to you,' said the policeman. 'Please come into this room.'

We went into a small room. 'It's about Carrie Black. About Carrie Black and her money,' said the policeman.

'What . . .' I didn't know what to say. 'What . . . what's happened?' I asked.

Gina didn't say anything. She didn't smile at me.

'We just want to talk to you, Mr Black. Please sit down,' said one of the policemen.

I sat down. The policemen sat down too. I looked at Gina, but she didn't look at me.

'Where did you get the money for these tickets?' asked the policeman.

'I . . . I . . .' I tried to speak.

'Maybe we have someone who can help you,' he said. He looked at the door and said, 'Come in, please!' The door opened and a girl walked in. A girl with blonde hair. I looked at her. I looked at her face. It was Carrie! She was alive!

'What . . . what, what are you doing here?' I asked.

The older policeman smiled at me. 'So, Mr Black,' he said, 'you know this young woman!'

Carrie smiled. It wasn't a nice smile. 'Oh, Brad,' she said, 'how stupid you are!'

Then Gina started talking.

'We saw a movie, Brad. You and me. It was called *Dead Money*. In the movie the woman kills her old, sick husband,' she said. 'You said it was a good idea. A good way to get money. I told you it was stupid.'

I looked at Gina. She talked again. 'Then I was at school one day, when you were "in Vancouver".' Gina smiled. It wasn't a nice smile. 'Carrie came to help with the children at the school. We started to talk and later we went for lunch.' She smiled at Carrie. 'I liked her.'

'We met a few times,' Carrie said, 'for coffee or lunch. I liked Gina and after a short time we were good friends. I told her about you . . . and she told me about her boyfriend. My husband and her boyfriend. They both had black hair and blue eyes. They both liked the movies. They were both called Brad . . .'

'Yes, then I started to think they were the same person,' Gina said, 'her husband and my boyfriend. The same Brad Black! Then Carrie showed me a photograph of her husband. It was you!'

'I told Gina about what happened on the roof,' said Carrie. 'You see, I was afraid. I knew you wanted to kill

me. I saw your face on the roof and I knew you wanted to kill me.'

'When I heard Carrie's story,' said Gina, 'I knew that you wanted to kill Carrie, just like in the movie. I couldn't love you after that!'

I looked at Gina. She was crying.

'Gina thought it was a good idea to leave you,' said Carrie. 'Just go. There were the Rosedale killings, so it was easy. We knew the police would think it was another killing. Three women dead. One of them, they didn't find her body. I was really afraid! I talked to Gina and then I decided to leave. You wanted to kill me!'

'So I found a small hotel in Toronto for Carrie,' said Gina, 'and Carrie stayed there. She didn't go out. She waited. I didn't say anything to you. I waited too. Until you said your rich aunt left you millions of dollars.'

Gina looked at me and the two policemen. 'Well, you know the end of the story,' she said.

'We just waited until you sent the money to Paris . . . my money,' said Carrie. 'I hate you! You never loved me! You only wanted my money!'

'But what did I do?' I asked. I looked at the policemen. 'I didn't kill anyone.'

'No, Mr Black,' said the policeman, 'but you tried to kill this young woman, you put the pen near the lake because you wanted the police to think that Carrie was dead, and then you stole Carrie's money. You are a stupid and dangerous man. You will go to prison for a long time.'

'So that was it. It was finished,' I said to Rufino. 'Gina didn't love me. She hated me. I thought I was intelligent, but I was stupid. So stupid! I tried to kill Carrie. And now

I'm here for five years!' I put my head in my hands and cried. Just like the day the police came and told me that Carrie was dead. But this time it was real. I wasn't acting. It wasn't a movie.

'But Brad,' said Rufino, 'this story could make you millions of dollars in Hollywood. You'll be a millionaire, and you don't need to kill anyone! You can have cars, houses, girlfriends,' said Rufino.

I looked at Rufino. 'No, it's too late, Joe,' I said.

'Too late, what do you mean, too late?' he said. 'This is a good story, maybe a great story! Prison too!'

'Look at this newspaper!' I said.

Joe looked at the newspaper on the table. He read the headline: 'Just Like A Movie Gets Oscar'. He looked at the photograph of Gina and Carrie. He looked at me.

'Yeah,' I said. 'It's my story . . . Gina and Carrie wrote my story and sent it to some movie producers. They made millions of dollars! Now they're rich, millionaires! And I'm here! In prison!'

'Wow!' said Joe. 'That really is a sad story, Brad,' he said.

'Yeah,' I said. 'A sad story . . . That's life. It's just like a movie . . .'